THE MAKING OF A
MAN OF GOD

Mark T. Barclay

First Printing 1993

ISBN 0-944802-19-2

Write:
Mark Barclay Ministries
P.O. Box 588, Midland, MI 48640-0588

CONTENTS

DEDICATION

I dedicate this book to Roy Hicks Sr., who has trained and equipped many ministers who now are the very voices that God will use to climax the ages.

I salute you in the Lord for your many years of accuracy in the Word and your precise leadership in our lives.

I am one of many preachers of righteousness who gratefully thanks you for being a true Father in the Faith.

CHAPTER 1
JESUS THE MAKER

"And Jesus, walking by the sea of Galilee, saw two brethren, Simon called Peter, and Andrew his brother, casting a net into the sea: for they were fishers.

And he saith unto them, Follow me, and I will make you fishers of men.

And they straightway left their nets, and followed him.

And going on from thence, he saw other two brethren, James the son of Zebedee, and John his brother, in a ship with Zebedee their father, mending their nets; and he called them."

Matthew 4:18-21

As a believer, one of the very first things you must learn is to deny yourself and follow thoroughly after Christ Jesus. In doing this, it doesn't take you long to realize that you cannot make yourself into a man or woman of God.

Jesus is the one who makes you into what He wants you to be. Without Him you cannot do it. It is impossible to walk in this Kingdom without Jesus being your Lord. You cannot serve Him any way you want to. You must serve Him the way He chooses. You must give up being your own master and become the servant of Jesus Christ.

In the above text we read how Jesus called some of His first disciples. I believe Jesus was impressed with the way these men were working with their hands. We see this same principle with the Prophet Elijah when he called Elisha to work with him. Elisha was working in the field for his father. I can't help but believe that this impressed both the prophet and his God.

In Matthew 4:19 Jesus called His men by saying (paraphrased), "Come and follow Me. . . ." This *following* was not a onetime deal or even for a short season. It was a call to divert their entire lives over to doing nothing but working with Jesus. *Following* is a lifelong process that one never completes. Praise God! We will talk about this some more in another chapter of this book.

Jesus also pronounced over His men a great promise. This promise of "I will make you" came to them before they even made a commitment to follow Him. The same is true with you. Jesus has committed Himself to do the same thing for you—MAKE YOU WHAT HE WANTS YOU TO BE—so you can do what He wants you to do.

You might just as well stop trying to make yourself something you're not. There is no use in seeking to be someone you are not, and there is no use in trying to fulfill a call you were never given.

Even if you knew exactly what He wanted you to be, you still do not possess the ability to turn yourself into it. Only the Lord can change you from the old you to the new you and cause you to fulfill your new call in life.

Jesus is saying to you today, "I will make YOU what I want you to be." "I will make you a real man of God." "I will make you a holy, sanctified believer." "I will make you a temple of My Holy Spirit." "I will make you a servant to fulfill My call." Jesus our Lord is wanting full reign in our lives to mold us, shape us, equip us, guide us, and anoint us.

THEY LEFT THEIR NETS

In verse 20 of this same text we see another powerful truth. This time the fishermen made the right move. They immediately left their nets and followed Him. Many people today have not at all left their nets. In fact, they simply have added the net of Christianity to their many other nets in life. In order for you to get the most out of Christianity, you must abandon yourself entirely and take on Christ. You cannot abandon part of yourself and put Christ in that small place. You must give up your life for His. It is not a partial commitment, rather a sold-out one.

> *"Then said Jesus unto his disciples, If any man will come after me, let him deny himself, and take up his cross, and follow me.*
>
> *For whosoever will save his life shall lose it: and whosoever will lose his life for my sake shall find it.*
>
> *For what is a man profited, if he shall gain the whole world, and lose his own soul? or what shall a man give in exchange for his soul?"*
>
> Matthew 16:24-26

Verse 21 of our Matthew 4 text also tells us the outcome of these men. "And going on from thence . . ." This is what I want for all of us. It's what the Lord wants also— that each of us goes on and on as we walk with Him. In this new Kingdom, the way up is down. You empty yourself and humble yourself, and the Lord lifts you up. You cannot *earn* promotion any longer, only the Lord can promote you.

"I am crucified with Christ: nevertheless I live; yet not I, but Christ liveth in me: and the life which I now live in the flesh I live by the faith of the Son of God, who loved me, and gave himself for me."

Galatians 2:20

CHAPTER 2
MENTORSHIP/INTERNSHIP

"After these things the Lord appointed other seventy also, and sent them two and two before his face into every city and place, whither he himself would come."

Luke 10:1

"But without a parable spake he not unto them: and when they were alone, he expounded all things to his disciples."

Mark 4:34

Jesus was the greatest Mentor who ever lived. He constantly was making His followers into real believers. He relentlessly trained, taught, and disciplined His men. They were some of the roughest cases but turned out to be "diamonds."

Jesus was not easy on people. He was very honest with them and spoke as one who had authority (Mark 1:22). One day at a well He exposed a woman's sin face-to-face with her (John 4:6-18). Another time Jesus was teaching and looked up to see a group of religious leaders in His meeting. He rebuked them publicly and even called them names. In fact, He used the lowest words in His vocabulary and called them serpents, snakes, and hypocrites (Matthew

23:33). On another occasion Jesus rebuked one of His disciples right in front of the others and even called him the devil (Mark 8:33).

Many times Jesus rebuked His men for doubt and unbelief. In fact right after He rose from the dead and appeared unto them, He rebuked them (Mark 16:14). I don't think this Jesus would make it in the ministry today. The Church would claim that He is too hard, has no love, has a spirit of control, is putting bondage on them, and is in it to build His own kingdom.

One time Jesus made a whip and literally *cleansed* the temple by running people right out of the church building . . . in front of everyone else (John 2:14-15).

These men whom Jesus mentored were used to a face-to-face relationship with their leader. They were convinced that the truth must prevail at all cost to human feelings and men's egos. They were not weak, frail, and sissified as are many of the men in our churches today.

These men also worked very hard and extremely long hours. They would work in the ministry of helps all day long and then sit in special classes with Jesus while He dealt with them more precisely. Many times, even after all this, they would be encouraged to pray through the night or help Him move to the next location. They were inexhaustible, as was their Leader.

> *"But without a parable spake he not unto them: and when they were alone, he expounded all things to his disciples.*
>
> *And the same day, when the even was come, he saith unto them, Let us pass over unto the other side.*

And when they had sent away the multitude, they took him even as he was in the ship. And there were also with him other little ships."

Mark 4:34-36

Jesus never seemed to tire by having these men around Him. Sometimes He would say things like, "Why do you reason among yourselves?" or "How long must I be with you?" or "Can't you even pray with Me for one hour?" but He never ran them off. Many leaders today seem to have hidden or withdrawn themselves and almost become untouchable. Many of them don't even have a single man who is groomed to take their place. They seem to be bothered by young (sometimes arrogant), questioning ministers around them.

"For though ye have ten thousand instructers in Christ, yet have ye not many fathers: for in Christ Jesus I have begotten you through the gospel."

1 Corinthians 4:15

Many ministers today have what the world calls a "stepchild" complex because they feel that they have not been fathered properly by these greater men. They feel that they get less attention than the *real* sons. Others have been reared in the ministry but by women (mothers) and not by the fathers. Mothers have their place, of course, but it isn't to *father*. Many of these younger men are wanting to be mentors themselves but just don't have the goods yet.

We must pray that the up-and-coming fathers of the faith will not fail to keep their heavy hand on the younger men and women of ministry ranks. Lord, help us to enjoy this kind of leadership as You tarry.

Please do not think that a young son of the faith or a

7

brother can mentor you. He can feed you and perhaps pastor you, but even he should be submitting himself to the true Bible elders.

> *"The elders which are among you I exhort, who am also an elder, . . .*
>
> *Likewise, ye younger, submit yourselves unto the elder. Yea, all of you be subject one to another, and be clothed with humility: for God resisteth the proud, and giveth grace to the humble."*
>
> 1 Peter 5:1, 5

Many ministers today have run all over the nation looking for someone who will lead them and help them, and most of them end up with the wrong man or inadequate leadership. This frustrates them even more, and eventually, as they discern that their new leader is really *taking* from them and not *helping* them, they break away and become loners.

Well, back to Jesus. He taught His men, rebuked them (even publicly), led them, prayed with them, gave them a place to serve, poured Himself into them, made them holy, and even left them an inheritance of full-time ministry.

INTERNSHIP

In order for a man to flow as mentor, he must have followers who want to be both students and interns. Without true internship, there is no true "mentorship" happening. Many people today want to "hook up" to leaders but not really submit themselves. They tell others who their father is but don't allow that man to speak into their life and ministry. They say they are a son in the faith but don't even come to the meetings or give of their finances. This is a great misinterpretation of the whole principle.

I want to remind you that it was Jesus who initiated this leadership/followership system in the Church. We are to follow His example precisely.

An intern is a student who is going beyond textbook study and beyond lecture and obtains experience from on-the-job training. He realizes that not only does he need knowledge and understanding, but he also needs personal tutoring to practice what he has been taught. Without this practical application and junior experience, he won't be trusted to do much and shouldn't be allowed to either. He needs a season to practice what he was taught under a senior minister's scrutiny, critcism, and correction.

There is a great difference between experience and seasoning. Many ministers have years of experience, but in all they have gone through, they didn't get too seasoned. In fact some became bitter, hurt, jealous, mad, resentful, unforgiving, hard, and worse. True interns are wanting desperately to work for a season under a father who not only has time in grade but also is seasoned. Amen.

Almost every major occupation has an internship program. The medical profession is a prime example of this. I wouldn't think of allowing a medical graduate student to operate on me if he hadn't gone on and worked under the close scrutiny of a senior doctor for a season. This is even more important in the ministry. Medical doctors deal merely with the human body, but the gospel minister is dealing with eternal things and the soul of man.

The reason we have so much arrogance in the pulpit today and so much malpractice in the ministry is because of a lack of this very principle. Ministries that try to function without Christ's plan for their entire character growth will almost always flounder, stagnate, default, and go defunct.

Real gospel leaders desire to help younger ministers develop their ministries. They put aside their own pleasures, and they pour their lives into others. They spend their lives maturing and equipping the believers who are around them—just the same as do true disciples. They present themselves constantly to be trained, matured, and equipped.

> *"David therefore departed thence, and escaped to the cave Adullam: and when his brethren and all his father's house heard it, they went down thither to him.*
>
> *And every one that was in distress, and every one that was in debt, and every one that was discontented, gathered themselves unto him; and he became a captain over them: and there were with him about four hundred men."*
>
> 1 Samuel 22:1-2
>
> *"These be the names of the mighty men whom David had . . ."*
>
> 2 Samuel 23:8

I have used these scriptures from the books of First and Second Samuel many times. They really display the two major elements of the making of men of God. First we see how David became a captain over his men, began to lead them, and actually turned them into some of God's most valiant men of war.

Second we see that men chose to follow David and actually sought him out to follow him. They gathered to him of their own free will. He didn't force his leadership on them or even go after them. They came to him.

In order to have preciseness in building men, you must have this kind of leadership and this same spirit of followership. In Adullam, men were turned from indebtedness, discontentment, and distressed lives to mighty men. This cave turned into their international headquarters, and David and his men were awesome and became known throughout the land. (You may want to get my new mini-book called *The Captain's Mantle* to study this text further.)

CHAPTER 3
WHAT IS A MAN OF GOD?

Through the years I've heard many people say, "I'm a holy man of God," "I am a mighty man of God," and I suppose some of those saying this truly were.

Many were speaking it (it seems) as sort of a faith confession; yet they were not living up to the things that they were confessing. There is a real confusion about this term "man of God."

I want you to look at Daniel as a good Bible example of what a real man of God is. He truly was a man of God. He walked like one, talked like one, lived daily like one, and refused to bow like one. Because of this, God honored his faith, life, and prayers.

> *"But Daniel purposed in his heart that he would not defile himself with the portion of the king's meat, nor with the wine which he drank: therefore he requested of the prince of the eunuchs that he might not defile himself."*
>
> Daniel 1:8

> *"And in all matters of wisdom and understanding, that the king enquired of them, he found them ten times better than all the magicians and astrologers that were in all his realm."*
>
> Daniel 1:20

You may want to open your Bible now and study the first eight verses of Daniel, chapter 1.

Notice that Daniel purposed in his heart that he would not be defiled. This is the first sign of a man of God. He purposes within himself that no matter how he's forced to live, no matter what closes in on him, or no matter what situation he finds himself in, he is determined to live godly and not let anything (people, food, drink, words, practices, or behavior patterns) cause him to corrupt or defile himself.

TEN TIMES BETTER

If you look further at verses 12 and 13, you'll see that Daniel challenged the system he was stuck in and the people who were over him in order to eat food that was not offered to idols. Daniel and his buddies actually came out ten times better. I believe this is equivalent and can be compared to Jesus' teaching about a thirtyfold, sixtyfold, or hundredfold Christian. You should compare yourself to the way that you lived before you met Christ; you might be surprised that you're doing okay after all.

Some Christians are one time better than they were when they were unsaved, some are two times better, some five times better, some eight times better, and some are actually ten times better. I would like to challenge you, right now, to lay down this book and your Bible and meditate on your life. Rehearse what you do, how you behave, how you feel, how you steward your money, etc., and see just how much better you really are compared to the way you were before you met Christ Jesus.

Have you accepted Christ but still live the way you

used to? Jesus wants you to be a man or woman of God. He wants and expects every one of us to be hundredfold Christians.

Open your Bible again, but this time go to Daniel, chapter 5, for our text. I'm going to give you a list of ten attributes of a man of God.

Here, King Belshazzar is really concerned about a hand that appeared to him and wrote, "*Mene, Mene, Tekel, Upharsin*" on the wall. In fact, verse 6 says that the joints of his loins were loosed, his knees smote one against the other, and his whole countenance changed. In verse 7 he called the astrologers and the soothsayers and all those known to interpret things, but they could not interpret this writing on the wall.

There are many people like this today who sincerely need interpretation for the things of their lives. They need a word from the Lord; yet they always turn to these kinds of people who do not really know the Lord at all.

I'd like to draw your attention to verse 11. I'd like you to underline in your Bible the first four words, "There is a man . . ." The king got upset with all of these soothsayers, astrologers, and prophesiers and was going to order them all killed, but the queen spoke up and said that there was a man in the kingdom who was a man of God.

TEN ATTRIBUTES OF A MAN OF GOD

Now I'm about to give you a list of ten things that define what a man of God is. If you'll read verses 11 and 12 in your Bible, you'll see them. I'll list the nine things mentioned there, as well as a tenth point.

A man of God is:

1. One who has the *Spirit of the Living God within him*.

2. One who has the *mind of Christ*. His mind is enlightened. He has understanding, and he has wisdom.

(In verse 12 you'll find the next six points.)

3. One who has an *excellent spirit*. He's humble, yet he's bold. He's teachable, yet he can teach. He forgives, yet he demands righteousness. He has an excellent spirit.

4. One who has *know-how*. He studies to show himself approved, and he knows the words of his God.

5. One who has *understanding*. In this understanding he has discretion, he has compassion for where people are at, and through this understanding, he can reach them.

6. One who has the *interpreting of dreams*. He can define what is and is not of God. He can help people out of the things that bombard their lives.

7. One who has the *showing of hard sentences*. Many people today are filled with questions. A man or a woman of God has the answers to those questions. They know the Word of the Lord; they know how to answer every man out of the hope that lies within them.

8. A *dissolver of doubts*. He's a hope builder and a

faith builder and an encourager to those who are in doubt.

(The ninth point is found in verse 17.)

9. One who *cannot be bribed or bought or persuaded with gifts to perform on the behalf of his God*. The king offered to give things to Daniel if he would interpret the saying on the wall. Daniel told the king to keep his gifts; yet he still interpreted the handwriting for him.

(In Daniel 1:8, we find the tenth point.)

10. One who *purposes in his heart not to be defiled*.

It's very important that you meditate in these things that I've written here in this chapter on "*What is a man of God?*" Without them, you may find yourself in the lions' den with no angels or in the enemy's furnace with no fourth man to dance with you. You may find yourself in the storms of life without Jesus walking on the water inviting you to come out.

I'd like to challenge you today not to be one time better, two times better, or even eight times better than you were before you met Christ. Go for it all, and be ten times better in this life, *because of Christ*, than you were before. Live right, purge yourself, be a clean vessel. I'd like to challenge you to get these ten principles describing a man of God working in your life. Practice holiness and righteousness, and you will see that as you enter the worst times of your life, *the Lord Jesus Christ will deliver you*!

CHAPTER 4
SEVENTY OUT—SEVENTY BACK

"After these things the Lord appointed other seventy also, and sent them two and two before his face into every city and place, whither he himself would come.

And the seventy returned again with joy, saying, Lord, even the devils are subject unto us through thy name.

And he said unto them, I beheld Satan as lightning fall from heaven.

Behold, I give unto you power to tread on serpents and scorpions, and over all the power of the enemy: and nothing shall by any means hurt you.

Notwithstanding in this rejoice not, that the spirits are subject unto you; but rather rejoice, because your names are written in heaven.

In that hour Jesus rejoiced in spirit . . ."

Luke 10:1, 17-21

After Jesus trained His men and spent time with them (on-the-job training), He sent them out to practice their ministries. They were sent out two by two and were to operate by their faith and inspiration. Jesus allowed them to take no purse and to rely on no script. Later He allowed

them both purse and script, but this was an internship practice run (Luke 22:35-36).

> *"And as ye go, preach, saying, The kingdom of
> heaven is at hand.*
>
> *Heal the sick, cleanse the lepers, raise the dead, cast
> out devils: freely ye have received, freely give.*
>
> *Provide neither gold, nor silver, nor brass in your
> purses,*
>
> *Nor scrip for your journey, neither two coats, neither
> shoes, nor yet staves: for the workman is worthy of
> his meat.*
>
> *And into whatsoever city or town ye shall enter,
> enquire who in it is worthy; and there abide till ye go
> thence.*
>
> *And when ye come into an house, salute it.*
>
> *And if the house be worthy, let your peace come upon
> it: but if it be not worthy, let your peace return to you.*
>
> *And whosoever shall not receive you, nor hear your
> words, when ye depart out of that house or city, shake
> off the dust of your feet.*
>
> *Verily I say unto you, It shall be more tolerable for the
> land of Sodom and Gomorrah in the day of judgment,
> than for that city.*
>
> *Behold, I send you forth as sheep in the midst of
> wolves: be ye therefore wise as serpents, and harm-
> less as doves."*
>
> Matthew 10:7-16

Jesus sent these seventy out to preach, teach, and heal.
They went by faith (believing for even a place to sleep) and

by memory of what they were taught. All seventy were sent out and all seventy returned.

That's right! All seventy returned. Seventy were sent out and seventy returned. In today's situation that would be a miracle. It would be more like seventy going out and sixty-eight returning. Sixty-eight would return, and Jesus would ask where the other two were, and the answer would be similar to this: "Well, Jesus, You know how You told us to go into the worthy homes and put our peace out, and if it stays, then we could lodge there, but if it returns, then leave? Well Rueben and Bart went into this widow woman's home (and man was she a widow), and they never came out. They said to tell You that they love You, Jesus, but will be too busy taking care of this widow to serve You in the ministry that You gave them."

Maybe today seventy would be sent out, but only sixty-five would come back. Jesus would ask them where the other five were, and they would answer something like this: "Well, Jesus, You know how You told us to go out by twos into every city and to live by faith and not take a purse? Well, our five missing brothers met a vitamin distributor and learned that they could earn much more money than what the ministry was providing, so they signed up. They said to tell You that they love You, Jesus, but they were just too busy earning good money to give themselves to the ministry You called them to. They said they would send You an offering when they could."

Maybe today seventy would be sent out and only sixty would come back. When Jesus would ask where the other ten were, they would answer something like this: "Well, Jesus, You know how You taught us to rejoice when we were persecuted and consider ourselves blessed because

21

our reward will be great in Heaven? Well, our ten missing brothers all got their feelings hurt and became offended because people didn't like what they preached. They said to tell You that they love You, Jesus, but they are just too hurt and burned out to obey the call You put on their lives."

But in Jesus' day, with His men, they were found coming and going from their leader. They stuck together, and they couldn't be moved away from the commitments they made to Christ.

Today many men are loners, and they are independent to the degree that they come when they want to and go where they want to. But in the early days of the Church, it wasn't this way. When the Apostle Paul wanted to join himself to the other disciples, he was rejected. However, when Barnabus stood up for him, they received him. The main point that Barnabus presented in Paul's defense was that he was found coming and going from the church and from among the believers (Acts 9:28).

Because Jesus was a mentor to His men, and they submitted willingly to Him, they had a strength that many of us don't know today. I believe, in Jesus' name, that we are going to awaken to these truths and change our ways.

CHAPTER 5
JESUS LOVES MINISTRY

"And the seventy returned again with joy, saying, Lord, even the devils are subject unto us through thy name.

And he said unto them, I beheld Satan as lightning fall from heaven."

Luke 10:17-18

Not only did these seventy intern ministers return from their mission to report to headquarters, but they did it with joy. They didn't come back with great horror stories, and they weren't burned out. They were thrilled that they were permitted ministry assignments, and they carried them out with glee.

Their report to Jesus was filled with faith and testimony. They bragged on His power and His name, and they rejoiced that it worked for them. They told stories about how the demons even were subject to them in His name. They were very satisfied to be in ministry and under the governments of their leader.

The reason many people today have burnout and no longevity in ministry is because they love their own life and keep it dear to themselves.

"But none of these things move me, neither count I my life dear unto myself, so that I might finish my course with joy, and the ministry, which I have received of the Lord Jesus, to testify the gospel of the grace of God."

Acts 20:24

Paul, the great apostle to the gentiles, had a revelation on life. He voiced it under the unction of the Holy Spirit when he wrote this scripture above, ". . . neither count I my life dear unto myself." This is it! You and I must not love our own life or even consider it dear to ourselves. Don't misunderstand. Life is dear, but it should be dear unto Christ. The Bible teaches us that we are not our own, but we've been bought with a price (1 Cor. 6:19-20). John taught us the same thing and declared that we overcome Satan by the blood of the Lamb, the word of our testimony, and not loving our lives even unto death.

MEN OF JOY

These seventy returned with joy. They found joy in what they were doing with Christ. Their speech was filled with excitement when they gave their testimonies. Even Jesus joined in the conversation with them. Jesus loves ministry.

That's right, Jesus loves ministry. He loves to work with you in ministry. He is totally consumed with the redemption of mankind. As you and I get involved with ministry, He works closer and closer with us. Not only do we find personal fulfillment and satisfaction, but He takes pleasure in us.

Jesus answered His men that day when they were

24

rejoicing in their dominion over demons. Jesus said, "I beheld Satan as lightning fall from Heaven." Praise God! Jesus loved the conversation and involved Himself immediately. I realize that He adjusted their perspectives in all this, but I can't help believe that Jesus was excited about their success in ministry. He had trained them, had sent them out, and was now enjoying their victory report.

I like to think that Jesus jumped right into the middle of their testimonies and told His. They were excited and so was He. They declared their dominion over demons; He declared his dominion over the devil himself. He was there, you know, when Lucifer was sent to the earth with the boot of the Father. Hallelujah!

I so covet the day when the end-time Church walks daily in this joy and when we return to receiving pleasure and satisfaction just from working in the church and fulfilling our ministries. I feel so much compassion for those who toil in the Kingdom and feel the pains of slavery as their reward.

> *"Because thou servedst not the Lord thy God with joyfulness, and with gladness of heart, for the abundance of all things;*
>
> *Therefore shalt thou serve thine enemies . . ."*
>
> Deuteronomy 28:47-48

If you want to be close to Jesus and commune with Him hourly, then you must go where He is and do what He does. Jesus is totally consumed with the work of the Church in the earth until its mission is complete. Once you get involved with this work, not only will you and Jesus be colaborers, but you will walk hand in hand. You will find personal fulfillment, satisfaction, and joy unspeakable.

CHAPTER 6
THE REAL POWER

*"Behold, I give unto you power to tread on serpents
and scorpions, and over all the power of the enemy:
and nothing shall by any means hurt you."*

Luke 10:19

Jesus was a master at bringing out the good in everything yet not letting any wrong slide by. When His men
returned from their ministry trip, Jesus rejoiced with them
in their testimonies, yet He kept their perspectives right.

Jesus agreed with His men that they were given power
to exorcise demons, but that wasn't the real power they
possessed. The real power they were given was not merely
to cast out demons or operate in any other ministry function. Don't misunderstand me. I know that the power to do
ministry supernaturally comes from the Lord Jesus, but
that was not the emphasis of what Jesus taught His men
that day.

Jesus taught His men that day that there was an even
greater power given them than to cast out demons. The real
power is all inclusive and not limited to one application.

Did you know that a man can cast out demons and

still not enjoy the full power of Christ? Look with me to Matthew 7:22-23.

> *"Many will say to me in that day, Lord, Lord, have we not prophesied in thy name? and in thy name have cast out devils? and in thy name done many wonderful works?*
>
> *And then will I profess unto them, I never knew you: depart from me, ye that work iniquity."*

You cannot tell whether a minister, church, or meeting is of Christ just because there are manifestations. In the text above they had prophesied, dealt with demons, and done mighty works all in the name of Jesus; yet they went to hell. Jesus recognized that they had done these works and displayed this power, but He never knew them. NEVER.

Don't be fooled today. Many are uprooting themselves to follow those who display power yet have no character. Crowds always follow signs, but when the crowds are the believers, then it is a shame to them. A perverse generation seeks a sign. Signs follow believers, not believers follow signs.

There is a false prophetic movement that Jesus warned us of. Now there is a true revival coming in these last days, but there is also a false one. Acts 2:17 tells us of a real prophetic outpouring that will reach even our young people. We do not despise prophesies nor do we quench the Spirit (1 Thess. 5:19-20).

In the seven gifts that God the Father gave the Church, the prophetic gift is included (Rom. 12:6-8), so is it in the five gifts that Jesus gave the Church (Eph. 4:11) and also the nine gifts that are of the Holy Spirit (1 Cor. 12:7-10).

No one will deny this. But there is still a false prophetic movement to look out for.

Jesus warned us of this in Matthew 24. He warned us of the perils of last-day living but really concentrated on the deception of those claiming to be prophets.

> *"And Jesus answered and said unto them, Take heed that no man deceive you.*
>
> *For many shall come in my name, saying, I am Christ; and shall deceive many."*
>
> Matthew 24:4-5
>
> *"And many false prophets shall rise, and shall deceive many."*
>
> Matthew 24:11
>
> *"Then if any man shall say unto you, Lo, here is Christ, or there; believe it not.*
>
> *For there shall arise false Christs, and false prophets, and shall shew great signs and wonders; insomuch that, if it were possible, they shall deceive the very elect."*
>
> Matthew 24:23-24

I want to remind you that even the Antichrist will do mighty wonders to the degree that he will deceive whole nations. In the trinity of Satan is a beast, FALSE PROPHET, and Antichrist. The very elect will be deceived, if possible.

Today you can see various forms and degrees of demonology. Most of it is overemphasized and not effective deliverance at all. Many people are being taken in by the false display of power and this ineffective soulful display of exorcism.

THE REAL POWER

Jesus told the seventy when they returned that the real power was the mental and physical strength and ability to overcome every obstacle of this life and to keep their Christianity. Paul had a great respect for his. (Read 1 Cor. 9:27 and Phil. 2:12.)

> *"Behold! I have given you authority and power to trample upon serpents and scorpions, and (physical and mental strength and ability) over all the power that the enemy* [possesses], *and nothing shall in any way harm you.*

Luke 10:19 (Amp.)

Once again I want to point out to you that the real power Jesus was talking about was the mental and physical ability to stay saved and live like a Christian. I've always said that the gospel of Jesus Christ is more than believable—it is livable. Jesus is with us every step of the way, empowering us over all mental warfare and fatigue, as well as physical attacks and burnout.

I know this sounds menial compared to performing miracles, but nonetheless it is the truth. Jesus taught that we would do greater miracles than He. He taught, so teaching can't be the greatest work. He preached, so preaching can't be it. He healed, so healing miracles can't be the greater work either. However, what didn't happen in that day was salvations and infillings of the Holy Spirit. These are greater works—the power and ability to get people saved and filled with the power to live as a Christian. Praise God!

Paul, in his final writings to his men, made this awesome proclamation:

"I have fought a good fight, I have finished my course, I have kept the faith . . ."

2 Timothy 4:7

He was declaring that he had fought a good fight here in this life. This is referring to the many storms of life that he faced that were designed to steal his Christianity. He also said that he had finished his course. Remember Acts 20:24, how this same Paul said that he would do this very thing? Nothing at all moved him off course. He finished his course in life. He also said that he had kept the faith. Praise God. This was Paul's declaration—that nothing in his entire life's experiences stole his faith in Jesus, that he was still a fervent Christian, and that he was on his way to Heaven.

Paul had this revelation that Jesus taught His men: that the real power was the mental and physical strength and ability to stay saved and serve actively through this whole life.

CHAPTER 7
MINISTERING WITH JESUS

I don't know what all it is about the ministry of Christ that can totally consume a man, but I know it does. In most cases this is great, but for some it is the very thing that seems to cause them trouble. How is that? I don't know, unless it's the work itself that ministers pour their lives into instead of their personal walk with Christ.

Many believers are working exhaustive hours in Christ's work, yet they never tire. Others burn out with just a little sacrifice after a short period of time. What is the difference? There are several reasons this could happen, but I'm going to deal with the biggest and most obvious one.

Ministry without Jesus is nothing but mere church work. Though mere church work is a noble burden and task, it isn't necessarily ministering to anyone. Our Lord Jesus wasn't so much involved in church work and service as He was in ministering life and healing to those who came to Him.

In our nation alone there are thousands of churchgoers who work very hard but really minister life to few. Isn't it a shame that all that time and money go into building their institution or organization rather than truly presenting the gospel to a hurting, suffering humanity?

> *"Behold, I give unto you power to tread on serpents and scorpions, and over all the power of the enemy: and nothing shall by any means hurt you."*

Luke 10:19

When the seventy intern ministers returned rejoicing and testifying about their powerful experiences, Jesus reminded them where their power came from. "Behold, I give unto you [this] power . . ." "Behold, **I** . . ." It was Jesus Himself who empowered these men. Their power was bestowed upon them while they were with Jesus. He was reminding them of this.

Their power would remain with them as long as they stayed in personal relationship with Jesus. Many people today do not realize this. They treat the anointing like it was a particular gift that was given them and that once you get it, it never leaves you. But this is a fallacy. It just isn't true.

Outside of a very intimate, personal relationship with Jesus Christ, there is no anointing. What anointing you received the last time you were with Him will eventually wane. You may not realize it, but it will. As it does, you will become less and less powerful and grow weaker and weaker. If you don't do something about this, you will eventually function by the power of a familiar spirit or simply by the arm of the flesh.

THE POWER COMES FROM HIM

Jesus reminded His men that their power came from

34

Him. It remained with them as long as they were with Him.

The Apostle Paul said that his first and upmost desire was to know Jesus and the power of His resurrection. This is the real hunger of men of God. They want to be with their First Love. They live daily to be close to the Lord and to seek His face for divine insights.

> *"And **he** goeth up into a mountain, and calleth unto Him whom **he** would: and they came unto **him**.*
>
> *And **he** ordained twelve, that they should be with **him**, and that **he** might send them forth to preach,*
>
> *And to have power to heal sicknesses, and to cast out devils . . ."*
>
> Mark 3:13-15

Notice in the above passage that I have marked the references that point out the person of Jesus. In these scriptures we learn that Jesus' call to His men was to *Him* and not to His ministry or work. Sure, after they had been with Him for a season, He sent them out to minister, but that was not the only intention of calling them.

The number one thing you and I are called to do is to be with Jesus. To fellowship with Him and to sit at His feet in prayer is our call. It includes conversations without ceasing and receiving our daily commandments.

> *"The former treatise have I made, O Theophilus, of all that Jesus began both to do and teach,*
>
> *Until the day in which he was taken up, after that he through the Holy Ghost had given commandments unto the apostles whom he had chosen:*
>
> *To whom also he shewed himself alive after his pas-*

> *sion by many infallible proofs, being seen of them*
> *forty days, and speaking of the things pertaining to*
> *the kingdom of God . . ."*
>
> Acts 1:1-3

It is still the heart desire of Jesus Christ to be with us and command us constantly. If we will give ourselves to the Word of God and prayer, we will hear His voice and ultimately stay on course. We should never have started the system of bringing things (projects, goals, building plans, etc.) to Christ, asking Him to bless them. We should stay before His face, on our knees, receiving our instructions and plans from Him.

We shouldn't be asking Him to bless our plans, visions, or goals; rather, we should be yielding ourselves to accomplish His. Our number one call is to be in the ministry of the Word of God and prayer—to be with Him. We should go before the Lord with an empty tablet and ask for daily commands and instructions.

> *"Then the twelve called the multitude of the disciples*
> *unto them, and said, It is not reason that we should*
> *leave the word of God, and serve tables.*
>
> *Wherefore, brethren, look ye out among you seven*
> *men of honest report, full of the Holy Ghost and wis-*
> *dom, whom we may appoint over this business.*
>
> *But we will give ourselves continually to prayer, and*
> *to the ministry of the word."*
>
> Acts 6:2-4

If you are going to be a success at all in your walk with Christ and enjoy your life in the church, you are going to have to learn to differentiate between what you do *for* Jesus and what you do *with* Him. You'll have to separate your kingdom activities from your personal, intimate time with Him.

CHAPTER 8
WHAT YOU ARE—WHAT YOU DO

"Notwithstanding in this rejoice not, that the spirits are subject unto you; but rather rejoice, because your names are written in heaven.

In that hour Jesus rejoiced in spirit . . ."

Luke 10:20-21

When Jesus told His men not to rejoice in the fact that they had cast out demons, He was not discrediting ministry. Jesus loves to demonstrate His power and prove His Word is true. He loves to confirm the Word that is preached. Jesus doesn't so much confirm a man's word, but He will confirm His Word.

Jesus reminded His men that they should rejoice in the fact that their names were written in Heaven and not just rejoice over ministry power. Remember our chapter on "The Real Power"? This is the heart of what Jesus was saying here to His men. He wasn't putting down ministry power; rather, He was exalting their eternal stance above it.

What was Jesus really saying? I'll tell you in Barclay terms. Jesus was really saying that what you are *NOW* is—and always will be—more important than what you do. Let me put it another way. What you do will never be as important as what you are. What you do is your ministry or your job description in Christ. What you are describes your relationship to Christ and your place in Heaven.

If you neglect what you are for what you do, you will sooner or later taint and defame all you've done. You must grow in the gift and ministry that Jesus gave you, but your character better grow with it. If your character matures faster than your gift, it won't hurt a thing. If your gift matures faster than your heart, then you will struggle to keep your ministry clean and your attitudes right.

You cannot live off of your own gift, but you have no choice in living after your own heart. Out of your heart flow the issues of life. Guard your heart, and you guard your entire life. The gift in you is for *others* to feed off of and to grow thereby. Your relationship with Christ is what *you* feed off of and grow thereby.

Many people neglect their relationship with Christ because they are so busy in ministry functions. They feel that they must keep their schedules and respond to everyone who puts a demand on them. This will keep you in the jeopardy zone and will eventually drain all your faith, joy, and unction. You will do your best to minister to others, but you yourself will be drying up, and your effectiveness will decrease gradually.

What you are *NOW* is—and always will be—more important than what you do!

One time a man said to me, "You are supposed to answer me that way because you are a pastor." I said, "No. Pastoring is what I do; a Christian is what I am." He said, "What?" I said, "I am a born-again, water-baptized, Spirit-filled believer who lives in his Bible and chases after the person of Jesus Christ. What I do is preach, teach, and heal God's people through the anointing Jesus gave me."

Never mistake the importance of concentrating on your relationship with the person of Jesus Christ rather than all the effort you put into your ministry duties. I've watched many ministers build their ministries (and some rather large) just to have the whole thing come tumbling down. Some of these men were masters at controlling the crowd (almost mesmerizing people with their eloquent speech) yet fell in the end. They could inspire others but couldn't keep their own house in order. Why? They put all their time and effort into their ministry functions but neglected to build their character.

What you are *NOW* is—and always will be—more important than what you do!

CHAPTER 9
NO SHORTCUTS IN GOD

*"Therefore leaving the principles of the doctrine of Christ, **let us go** on unto perfection; not laying again the foundation of repentance from dead works, and of faith toward God,*

Of the doctrine of baptisms, and of laying on of hands, and of resurrection of the dead, and of eternal judgment.

And this will we do, if God permit."

Hebrews 6:1-3

*"As newborn babes, desire the sincere milk of the word, **that ye may grow** thereby . . ."*

1 Peter 2:2

"He that descended is the same also that ascended up far above all heavens, that he might fill all things . . ."

"And he gave some, apostles; and some, prophets; and some, evangelists; and some, pastors and teachers;

*For the **perfecting** of the saints, for the work of the ministry, for the **edifying** of the body of Christ:*

Till we all come in the unity of the faith, and of the

*knowledge of the Son of God, **unto** a perfect man, **unto** the measure of the stature of the fulness of Christ:*

*That we henceforth be **no more children**, tossed to and fro, and carried about with every wind of doctrine, by the sleight of men, and cunning craftiness whereby they lie in wait to deceive;*

*But speaking the truth in love, **may grow up** into him in all things, which is the head, even Christ . . ."*

Ephesians 4:10-15

Notice the words that I underlined in the previous verses. I want to draw your attention to the many times the scriptures refer to us growing up in Christ. Many people think that all there is to being a Christian is to be born again, but that is not what Jesus taught. He said you must be born again but never said that that is all you must do. It is only the start of your eternal walk with God.

God's plan for our life is not complicated. He wants us to be born of His Spirit and grow up in Him. It is the will of God that we grow in all areas of our life and then fulfill our ministry of helping other people do the same.

Jesus inserted a system for growth and ministry, and there are no shortcuts or ways around it. I don't know why so many people think that they can arrive at a lofty place in Christ when they cheat the system all along the way.

You cannot serve Jesus the way you want to. You must serve Him the way He says. You are not your own, you've been bought with a price. He is the King, you are the subject. He snaps—you jump, not you snap—He jumps.

If you will study the Gospels and the epistles of the

New Testament, you can easily see the plan of growth that Jesus instituted in the Church. There are four main parts to it: 1) Conversion, 2) Epistleship, 3) Discipleship, and 4) Ministry. I want to help you understand each phase of this Christian growth system.

CONVERSION

CONVERSION is the first phase of Christian life and growth. In order for you and me to walk with God and do the work of ministry, we must be converted from all our ways. Conversion must take place or else you will sooner or later shame yourself in default and probably ultimately hurt the reputation of the kingdom of God.

We call these people converts. They are the ones who have been born again and desire to follow Christ with the rest of their life. They come to church services and sit under the teaching ministries to learn the rules and principles of this new life. They sit under the pastoral ministries to be fed and led forward out of their old lifestyles into the new.

It isn't enough that someone desires this conversion in their life. Desire alone will not keep you alive and well, as it will not make you pure. You must do something to walk on with Christ.

Converts should be taught that conversion takes time and usually a lot of sacrifice. You can be forgiven on the spot, but it will take time to convert all your ways. Your lifestyle, habits, practices, beliefs, attitudes, convictions, etc., must all be slowly changed to the new life.

You have sins, practices, habits, and even some friends

that you must get delivered from. This does not happen overnight. Yes, inside you are brand new and old things have passed away but not so on the outside. You must work out your salvation with fear and trembling (Phil. 2:12).

In order to be converted from all your ways, you will need your Bible, a Spirit-filled church family, a new set of friends who serve God, your pastor, and a lot of prayer and fasting.

Once you have been purged, delivered, healed, and renewed, you can go on in your Christian walk. Let me remind you that there is no sense in going on from here if you are going to drag old habits and ways with you. These sins alone will just bring you back to this point one day.

> ". . . And said, Verily I say unto you, Except ye be converted, and become as little children, ye shall not enter into the kingdom of heaven."
>
> Matthew 18:3

EPISTLESHIP

EPISTLESHIP is the second phase of Christian life. After a person has been converted from his old ways, then he can go on to this season of growth. Please note that this isn't *apostleship,* rather *epistleship.* The word epistle simply means letter. People are watching your walk in this life, whether you realize it or not, even if you don't want to admit it.

This is the time in your walk with Christ that you have the sense of accomplishment because you have been cleansed from the old way, and now you can live what you've learned. The gospel of Christ is more than believable, it is livable. Jesus brought us these things that we might live them and not just memorize them.

Never make the lethal mistake of thinking that just because you know something, you are doing it. Knowing it is important, but doing it is a whole different matter. Many people today misinterpret this very thing.

Living epistles are people who can now live the gospel every day of their lives. They aren't just church-goers who put on a white-washed show when they are around other churchgoers, but they are people who can live it every day of their lives. There is something wrong when others only know we are Christians when we tell them.

A real epistle of Christ can be followed and observed even in his private times and never be caught doing unscriptural things because he never does them. This is a man who has been converted from his old ways and has now begun to live out the life of Christ.

> *"Ye are our epistle written in our hearts, known and read of all men . . ."*
>
> 2 Corinthians 3:2

DISCIPLESHIP

DISCIPLESHIP is the phase of Christian life where you present yourself ready for discipline. This is the time where you crave to obtain the disciplines of the Christian walk in your everyday life. You have been converted from your ways and lived a season as an epistle of Jesus Christ, and now you are ready to walk and serve with preciseness.

There are several areas of discipleship that a good mature student covets for his life. The first area is self-discipline. This is a must if you are going to go on in God. Only you can discipline yourself in certain areas of your life. The more you apply self-discipline to your life, the less you will need governments from your leaders.

Self-discipline causes you to study, pray, abstain from evil, be prompt, keep your word, etc. Self-disciplined men get up on time, and they govern themselves closely. This is a great part of preparing yourself for ministry and service in the Kingdom.

Almost all converts and most epistles have little (if any) self-discipline. However, once you have passed through these areas of growth, you can become a disciple. A disciple is a student who is now ready to have discipline applied to his life. Many people who think they are disciples really are not.

Many people, thinking they are disciples, want to do work in levels that mature Christians work in; yet they are too immature to carry it out. They become offended or hurt, and many of them faint in heart and quit.

If a pastor appoints a convert or epistle to fulfill the position of a disciple, he will normally smart or sting for it. You just can't expect undisciplined and immature people to walk in this kind of preciseness and under such demand.

If the pastor tells a convert to come to the church building at 9 a.m. to prepare the building for service, he had better call at 8 a.m. to remind him and check again at 8:30 to assure that the job is done. No offence intended, but a convert is just not a disciple. If a disciple is told to be there at 9 a.m. to prepare the building, he never has to be checked on. The pastor could arrive at one minute before nine, and the work assignment will be done just as expected. This is the difference between disciples and those trying to be.

There are many illustrations that I could use here, but I think you get the message. Converts are beginners and learners, epistles are the purged ones who live it, and disciples are the students who have become obedient and precise in all they do.

Discipline is also applied to your life through the Holy Spirit, the Word of God, and your leadership. A true disciple can handle open rebuke, correction, and the pressure that comes from spiritual attacks and tribulations. Things don't move disciples, not even if they are filled with criticism, pressure, stress, hurt, and humiliation.

MINISTRY

MINISTRY is the fourth and final phase of your Christian walk. Once you have been converted from the old life, lived as an epistle, and fulfilled discipleship, you are ready to fulfill your ministry. It doesn't matter so much exactly what your ministry is as it does how you fulfill it. To be an apostle is no greater than being an usher if that is what Jesus has commissioned you to do.

Many people want to move from conversion to apostleship or full-time ministry. I've watched some of these men even grow to fame but falter in their private lifestyle. If you can't live it but only preach it, you are nothing but sounding brass and a clanging cymbal.

The rest of us need you desperately today. We need you in full operation of your ministry. It is a crucial day, and every one of us must obey Christ and be workers together with Him without being ashamed. We covet to have you in the fullness of your ministry but not at the sake of your life.

Many people who have coveted a ministry (not their own) or even entered their given ministry too early, have ended in shipwreck and painful despair. There is no short-cut in God—no meritorious promotions. Each man must prove himself and his own work. This is the system of the kingdom of God.

MULTITUDER

All of us came into the Kingdom through the multi-tude. We came out of the world and began to follow Jesus. The "multituders" are those who follow the crowd as they follow Jesus. The size of a meeting can really impress them, and they always come to watch the fish and loaves be multiplied and the sick receive miracles, but they leave as soon as possible. They follow the dust clouds caused by the masses.

I could not stay too long as a "multituder" because I would notice that the seventy were closer to Jesus and spending more time with Him. I would notice the correc-tion they were getting that I wasn't and the special training also. I couldn't help but notice that they were given certain assignments by Jesus and were allowed to practice their ministry under His scrutiny.

THE SEVENTY

I would just have to be part of this seventy group. My hunger for Jesus would drive me closer to Him and away from the "multituders" whom I once belonged to. I'm not a greedy man, so I wouldn't try to replace one of the seventy; rather, I'd say, "Couldn't there be seventy-one, Jesus? I know that I'm supposed to be part of this more mature and disciplined group."

THE TWELVE

It wouldn't take me long as one of the seventy before I would hunger to be one of the Twelve. I would notice that the Twelve were closer to Jesus and were spending more time with Him. I would notice the correction they were getting that I wasn't and the special training also. I couldn't help but notice that they were given certain assignments by Jesus and were allowed to practice their ministry under His scrutiny.

I would just have to be part of this Twelve. My hunger for Jesus would drive me closer to Him and away from the seventy whom I once belonged to. I'm not a greedy man, so I wouldn't try to replace one of the Twelve; rather, I'd say, "Couldn't there be thirteen, Jesus? I know that I'm supposed to be part of this more mature and disciplined group."

THE THREE

It wouldn't take me long as one of the Twelve to notice that Jesus always called upon three of us to go raise the dead and experience things like the Transfiguration. I would just have to be with Peter, James, and John as Jesus called upon them to do exploits with Him.

I would notice that the three were closer to Jesus and

spending more time with Him. I would notice the correction they were getting that I wasn't and the special training also. I couldn't help but notice that they were given certain assignments by Jesus and were allowed to practice their ministry under His scrutiny.

I would just have to be part of this three. My hunger for Jesus would drive me closer to Him and away from the Twelve whom I once belonged to. I'm not a greedy man, so I wouldn't try to replace one of the three; rather, I'd say, "Couldn't there be four, Jesus? I know that I'm supposed to be part of this more mature and disciplined group."

THE CLOSEST ONE

My hunger to be close to Jesus would cause me to notice the communion that John enjoyed with Him. I would immediately crave to have that kind of relationship with Jesus. I wouldn't be jealous of John nor would I want his place. I wouldn't ask Jesus to replace John with me but to add me to this relationship. I would say, "Jesus, You have two shoulders, and John only has his arm around one. Can I have the other?"

I'm sure you have this same driving hunger to have an intimate relationship with Jesus Christ. The more you walk with Him, the more you want to. The more you serve Him, the more you want to. The more you abandon this life for His, the more you want to. I keep falling in love with Him over and over and over and over again!

CHAPTER 10
HOW TO LAUNCH YOUR MINISTRY

Did you know that there are businesspeople who come into churches to reap but never sow? Did you know that there are ministers who go out of churches and come and go from churches but never do anything to help build the work? They just take from it, using the ministry for a launching pad or for a source center. Eventually these businesspeople will grow broke because they come to take instead of give. Eventually these ministries will fall apart. I don't care how well they start out—eventually they'll fall apart. They are takers and not givers. They will reap what they sow.

I've watched them over the years. One young man left a church, and even though his pastor said not to go yet, he said he was going anyway. He went across town and started a church, and he committed that he wouldn't invite anyone in that church to go with him.

Listen, if a pastor gave you any kind of position of authority, favor, or privilege to do anything, and you don't move far enough away, the people who have attached themselves to you are going to go with you or at least be tempted to. It doesn't matter if you say I told them not to come. You shouldn't have moved so close. It's like Abraham and Lot. Abraham said [paraphrased], "There's not enough room here for both of us to prosper, so choose where you want to go and journey there." The Bible says that Lot looked afar off and found a valley that was close to Sodom and Gomorrah and moved there. I'm talking about sowing in direct relationship to reaping.

Do you know what happened to the young man? Several years went by, and that whole thing fell apart. That young preacher called me and asked me to come help him. I said, "I want to help you because I love you—I'm a man of grace and a man of love—and I want to help you. But for the record, before I come, I want you to remember the day that you sat in my office and I told you to your face that that which is born of the flesh is flesh, and it never becomes Spirit. I told you that day that you could not start a church that close to the home church because different people would be drawn with different emotions, because not all people are led by God, and though you didn't invite them, I told you that day that you'd ruin and hurt that other work. Now you've ruined and hurt it, and you've pretended for years that you didn't, and here you sit, and the whole thing has blown up in your lap. Now, I'll come and help you, but before I do, I want you to say to your God that you were warned and you did wrong and that you repent for birthing this thing in the flesh because you were a young preacher who wanted a paycheck and didn't want to work your secular job anymore. Now if you repent, I'll come and help you."

So he did. He called me back and told me that he repented and that he told his wife and his people that he made it right. I told him I'd come help him but that there was absolutely no way to make the thing spiritual and that I wouldn't pretend with him. This thing was birthed in the flesh, and it will always be flesh. Call it a church, call it a fellowship, call it an outreach center, call it whatever you want to call it, but it is a mess of flesh—Heaven knows it, and even demons are drawn to it, and every goofy person alive is going to want to come and have a ministry in that thing. Flesh draws flesh. I said, "I'll come help you close it down and make it right in your city and break the power of the demons that you've given place to all these years because you did it wrong in the name of God. Then I'll help you get in a ministry someplace where you'll flourish." He said, "Come on, let's do it." Now he's flying high, but the other thing fell apart. The sad part of this story is that neither of the churches are functioning today. They're both wasted, and the doors are closed. Don't fool yourself. God said He would not be mocked on this thing. Whatever a man sows, that's what a man is going to reap. Start out in the flesh—end in flesh. It may look and sound spiritual to others, but it'll only last a short time.

A WRONG EXAMPLE

To come to a church and receive what that church gives you is okay, but to take from it is wrong, even if you're being raised up there. If you're one of the up-and-coming businesspeople or up-and-coming ministers, the church wants to help you. We have ways to help you, but don't take from us. You'll hurt yourself. We're not going to prosecute you, but don't come in here and use our phone thinking that we owe you something because you're starting a ministry out of our church, and now our whole congregation should not only pay our phone bill but yours too. The minute you declared that you were sent out of here, you should've cut the strings from the source here and said, I'm mature enough to believe God for myself. I don't need anything you've got.

A GOOD EXAMPLE

As we sent out one young minister, we blessed him, we helped him, and every so often we sent offerings. Once in a while Vickie and I send money. We pray for him—he's our partner, I talk to him on the phone—I'm still his pastor, they'll be back here to visit, and they'll always be family. They're doing it as right as they know how. We're helping them as right as we know how. Yet when he left, I said, "You live on your faith now, buddy. The apron strings are cut. You've been weaned. If God called you to that city, God will give you that city, not Barclay. You get no meetings on my name. You go out and birth this thing in the Spirit just like we did this one in Midland. If God has sent you and you know how to believe God and you do what I've taught you to do, this thing will sprout up and grow for you." He went out and has never asked for a thing, other than for prayer. We're partners, and we do *sow* to him, but he doesn't *take.*

A WRONG EXAMPLE

It would be wrong for a businessperson to attend our church and start volunteering for things just to gain our mailing list so that on the side (from his office) he can write you and ask you for support or sell you his little thing that he's selling. It's wrong. I'm not offended by it (I know a wolf when I see one), but if you're one of these business-people, you're not going to reap anything but trouble. You're sowing the wrong kind of seed. You're not receiving what we're giving. You're taking what you can get.

You beginning preachers listen to me. I'm going to tell every single one of you right to your face: Don't sit here and take from this ministry, because it will cost you severely—later. I know what I'm talking about. Whatever the church gives you, whatever the leadership of the church designates to you—go ahead and take it. Rejoice over it. Be thankful and grateful and humble about it, but don't steal our mailing list. Don't go visit all the people while you're here growing up in the ministry and write down their phone numbers and addresses and then go back to your own office and mail them letters asking for support—you're stealing. You might say, ". . . but they're my friends." That's even more reason why you shouldn't proselyte and steal and work underneath the system and make yourself look like a beginner when we've sent you out, and you should do right. I pray for these novices, that they don't hurt themselves. My attitude is as though I gave it to them though I know they took it. Nonetheless, I want them to be blessed. Yet, the Lord tells me He won't bless them—they're lying, they're cheating, they're not giving to the ministry, they're taking from it.

LISTEN TO THIS

Did you know that to be raised up and sent out is the Book of Acts and the Holy Ghost, but to rise up and go out is the flesh and the devil? One man told me he was leaving whether I blessed him or not. I told him I was blessing him because he was going to need it—big time! I said, "You can be cocky if you want to, but this church is blessing you. You're going out, and I can tell you're going out whether I like it or not, and three months from now you're going to need every bit of blessing this church can put on you." They're kids. Some of them don't know what they're getting into. They don't know the hell, the warfare, and the demonizing that goes on. Some of them fly high and still don't know.

Let's say a person who feels called to preach attends our church and goes to school here, serves a while, and learns some things about ministry. But while he's here serving with us, he is thinking in the back of his mind, I have my own ministry. So he goes to our Publications Department and coerces our artist (and the people whom I pay to do our ministry) into making his business cards, advertising his meetings with fliers, and getting *his* tape albums ready. The leadership never offered that, though he's *taking* it. The church is paying for it. While he's here, he makes sure that he gets a copy of all of the Bible school curriculum. He does this while he's here, because when he leaves, he's going to have to have all these things, and bless God, he doesn't want to get them from God on his own, he may as well take them from us. When he gets everything he wants (his business cards, advertisement brochure, curriculum, etc.) that the church paid for, it still is not enough. He's going to keep a connection, because while he was here, he gathered your names and numbers so that once he gets into his own "ministry," he can write you for prayer and financial support.

Are you smart enough to know that a house divided against itself cannot stand? Do you know who's going to get the most out of a church ministry? The guy who toils and labors and works in the Helps Ministry and goes out preaching in between services and comes back and brings his tithes into the house of God and brings his offerings in here and reports for duty and mingles with the brethren and doesn't act like a big shot. That guy is going to reap out of here, and he's going to have more than enough, because the people are going to say, "He's not hurting and taking and splitting the house, he's adding to it with whatever he's got. He's been raised up here and sent out . . ." I'm talking about principles that are violated everywhere.

There's no way an average church can support five or six different ministries and pay for all this and pay for all that and print all this and print all that and do all this and do all that. Do you know what would happen to a church if all the ministers had four armorbearers who traveled with them? The armorbearers would stop coming to church because they were out traveling with the ministers; and if they were in town, they'd be tired so they would go fishing or hunting or lie in the grass and not even come back to report for duty. "Well we've been out preaching, we're tired. You don't know what we've been doing." I know what I've been doing, and I still report for duty here, because I'm a man of God. I'm not afraid to tell this to preachers because I've learned that your future is in exact, direct relation to what you sow.

When I started out in the ministry, I worked a secular job, I went to Bible school, and Vickie and I worked more than what most of the associate pastors worked. Our babies grew up under the pews. I didn't have one helper for five to six years—not one helper. I had no babysitter, I had no armorbearers (even though there were people around me), but we felt called. We didn't break down, we didn't fly high, we didn't compare ourselves with our pastor like "we're equal with him." We stayed humble and submitted, knowing that the way up in the Kingdom is down, that if you want your own, you take care of another man's first. You take care of another man's first but don't get your own by using his ministry as a springboard or a launching pad.

LAW OF ACCUMULATION

Many young ministers want to have, in one year, what seasoned ministries took years to accumulate (a working staff, buildings, machinery, promotion, a following, a donor base, etc., that are all inclusive in this law of accumulation).

Even though some young preachers do *prosper* quickly, it is a flash of prosperity and not true accumulation. Most of them can't handle the success or the prosperity. They are immature in character though VAST in size or possessions.

The statement "God gives you what He can trust you with" should be spoken carefully. Though there is truth here, many mistake the real meaning. You have to remember that there is such a thing as unjust gain. I'll guarantee you that God is not the one giving to many of these novices and loose-living preachers. Neither does He trust them. Don't count all increase as God's blessing. Prosperity, growth, and prestige may be cancerous and tumorous and not at all descriptive of spirituality or holiness.

BASIC ELEMENTS TO LAUNCHING
YOUR MINISTRY

1. James 5:7-8

WAIT—until it's the timing of the Lord. Do not let the novice-like zeal drive you away. Mature people are sent out by leaders. They don't run away from home. You will never regret doing it right and in the right season.

2. 2 Tim. 2:15; 1 Tim. 4:15-16

STUDY—because you cannot impart something you don't have. Neither can you teach something you don't know. Preparation is vital to ministerial survival. Learn the five Ps (**Proper Planning Prevents Poor Performance**), and stick with them. One of the biggest mistakes you can make is overrating yourself. Peter did this. Jesus prayed for him that his faith would not fail, but Peter didn't listen. Jesus instructed him that he should encourage the brethren "when he returned." Peter may not have denied Christ if he would have taken warning that day. Don't assume you are ready. Ask Jesus and your pastor to evaluate you.

3. Acts 6:2,4

FAST AND PRAY—so that you guarantee your life and ministry are—and always will be—in line with God and His Word. Don't just develop your communication skills. Many have become great *pulpiteers* but live a life of undeveloped character. You must spend time with God and live a life of fasting. This will keep you lean and clean as well as in the perfect will of God.

4. Acts 13:1-4; 2 Tim. 2:3-4

SLOWLY CUT STRINGS—don't be a spurt. Be sure you are sent out and blessed. Never do anything abruptly. Though you cut most of your ties with the local setting, you begin a brand new level of relationship with your pastor and the local church. Don't force this, let it develop. Never burn bridges. Always fortify relations with your fathers in the faith.

5. 1 Thess. 5:11-13; 2 Tim. 1:1-2

COMMUNICATE TO YOUR PASTOR—build a partnership. Your relationship with your pastor should now increase. It also should mature—a less pastor-sheep relationship and a more colaborer relationship should develop. You should make the transition from one of the flock to one of the five-fold. You'll have to adjust your relations with the sheep now and almost stop all fellowship with them. If you can't do this, you are probably not mature enough or ready to be launched into your own ministry. Stay in even closer touch with your pastor. You will need him now more than ever.

6. 1 Thess. 4:11; 2 Cor. 13:5 (NKJV)

GO BY FAITH—cut the apron strings. Believe God. Leave everything and everyone behind. Don't live in a man's house and then take his belongings or one of his children when you move on. If God is sending you, then *He* can provide for you. Prove your own work.

7. Gen. 13:8-11; Rom. 15:20

GO FAR ENOUGH AWAY—do not build on another man's foundation. God is not a church splitter. He doesn't send people to an area to duplicate efforts, nor does He cause someone to leave a ministry and go across the street to start a new one. Either stay connected—coming and going—or separate yourself with lots of miles.

PRAYER OF SALVATION

YOU CAN BE SAVED FROM ETERNAL DAMNA-TION and get God's help now in this life. All you have to do is humble your heart, believe in Christ's work at Calvary for you, and pray the prayer below.

"Dear Heavenly Father:

I know that I have sinned and fallen short of Your expectations of me. I have come to realize that I can-not run my own life. I do not want to continue the way I've been living, neither do I want to face an eter-nity of torment and damnation.

I know that the wages of sin is death, but I can be spared from this through the gift of the Lord Jesus Christ. I believe that He died for me, and I receive His provision now. I will not be ashamed of Him, and I will tell all my friends and family members that I have made this wonderful decision.

Dear Lord Jesus:

Come into my heart now and live in me and be my Savior, Master, and Lord. I will do my very best to chase after You and to learn Your ways by submit-ting to a pastor, reading my Bible, going to a church that preaches about **You**, and keeping sin out of my life.

I also ask You to give me the power to be healed from any sickness and disease and to deliver me from those things that have me bound.

I love You and thank You for having me, and I am eagerly looking forward to a long, beautiful relation-ship with You."

Other Books by Mark T. Barclay

Beware of Seducing Spirits

This is not a book on demonology. It is a book about people who are close to being in trouble with God because of demon activity or fleshly bad attitudes.

Building a Supernatural Church

A step-by-step guide to pioneering, organizing, and establishing a local church.

Charging the Year 2000

This book will alert you and bring your attention to the many snares and falsehoods with which Satan will try to deceive and seduce last-day believers.

Enduring Hardness

God has designed a program for His saints that will cause each one to be enlarged and victorious. This book will challenge your stability, steadfastness, courage, endurance, and determination and will motivate you to become a fighter.

How to Avoid Shipwreck

A book of preventive medicine, helping people stay strong and full of faith. You will be strengthened by this book as you learn how to anchor your soul.

How to Relate to Your Pastor

It is very important in these last days that God's people understand the office of pastor. As we put into practice these principles, the Church will grow in numbers and also increase its vision for the world.

How To Always Reap a Harvest

In this book Dr. Barclay explains the principles that make men successful and fruitful. It shows you how to live a better life and become far more productive and enjoy a full harvest.

Improving Your Performance

Every leader everywhere needs to read this book. It will help tremendously in the organization and unity of your ministry and working force.

Preachers of Righteousness

As you read this book, you will be both edified and challenged to not only do the work of the ministry but to do it with humility, honesty, and godliness.

Sheep, Goats, Wolves

A scriptural yet practical explanation of human behavior in our local churches and how church leaders and members can deal with each other.

The Sin of Familiarity

This book is a scriptural study on the most devastating sin in the body of Christ today. The truths in this book will make you aware of this excess familiarity and reveal to you some counter-attacks.

The Sin of Lawlessness

Lawlessness always challenges authority and ultimately is designed to hurt people. This book will convict those who are in lawlessness and warn those who could be future victims. It will help your life and straighten your walk with Him.

The Making of a Man of God

In this book you'll find some of the greatest, yet simplest, insights to becoming a man or woman of God and to launching your ministry with accuracy and credibility. The longevity of your ministry will be enhanced by the truths herein.

The Remnant

God has always had a people and will always have a people. Dr. Barclay speaks of the upcoming revival and how we can be those that are alive and remain when our master returns.

Mtg 7/6/95

① Minister In Training ③
② Minister — or Licensed Ministers
               Credentials

Need Ministerial Card
      Board of Bishops Mtg. — Nov.
⑤ Presbytery (ministerial) (12)
④ Ordained Minister — 1st Sun. in Nov.

List of Presbytery in next mtg.

Apostolic Ministerial Fellowship

Open Door Ministry
Evangelist Antoinette Shuey
P.O. Box 61
Germantown, Maryland 20875
301-916-6882